ONCE A WEEK FITNESS FOR WOMEN

A Non-Aerobic Muscle Toning Programme for Women of All Ages

by

Barbara Roberton

THORSONS PUBLISHING GROUP
Wellingborough * New York

First published April 1986
Second Impression May 1986

British Library Cataloguing in Publication Data

Roberton, Barbara
    Once a week fitness for women: a non-aerobic
    muscle toning programme for women of all ages.
    1. Exercise for women 2. Physical fitness for
      women   I. Title
    613.7'1'088042   RA781

    ISBN 0-7225-1261-9

Printed and bound in Great Britain

Dedicated to Alan, Nicola, Katy,
and Dizzy

Contents

Introduction

Once a Week Fitness is for women of all ages, shapes, and sizes. Our appearance says a lot about the way we look after ourselves and a good figure can be more of an asset than a pretty face. Feeling fit and looking good doesn't have to mean constant pounding with exercise or starving. It does mean treating the body with respect, eating sensibly and exercising regularly, at least *once a week*.

This book is to help you tone up your muscles, firm up any 'flab' and have that wonderful glow that comes from feeling fit and healthy.

How to Start

Instead of spending more and more money on clothes and make-up, which are only disguises, take a good look at yourself and make a list of your good points and your bad points. Beauty doesn't mean a skinny 'model' type figure or hours spent in front of the mirror. It comes from within: as the saying goes, 'Healthy mind, healthy body'. So you don't have to be a film star, a teenager, or under nine stone; you need determination, a little will power, and the confidence to stand up straight and have pride in the way you look and feel.

What Kind of Exercise?

There are many ways of exercising — walking, running, swimming, dancing, or cycling — but it is no use doing something you hate just because you think it will do you good. The exercises in this book are non-aerobic, muscle-toning exercises based on many years experience as a dancer and a teacher of ballet, tap, and keep fit classes. All the exercises should be done to music. Movement to music is as much a part of our existence as eating and drinking. It is a natural human reaction and our inbuilt sense of rhythm makes the exercises enjoyable and satisfying.

Benefits of Exercise

By following the exercises in this book with determination and will power and of course a sensible diet you will soon find that:

- your tummy is flatter
- your thighs and bottom firmer
- your waist noticeably trimmer
- your posture elegant and upright

You will also see an improvement in your skin, hair, and eyes and feel generally healthier and happier.

Think Fit

Your attitude towards yourself is very

important. Have a positive attitude and it will show in the way you walk and stand. It will also show in your face. You are your own best friend or your own worst enemy. Don't dwell on petty irritations; life is too short for that. Smile and enjoy life. It's amazing how infectious a smile can be!

Make Time to Exercise

Get into the habit of exercising. Make it as much a part of your routine as putting on make-up or washing your hair.

You spend all your life growing old; take a little time to keep young, fit, and healthy. *You owe it to your body*. Use everyday tasks as a form of exercise, and they too will seem more enjoyable.

Learn to Relax

We have to learn to relax and use the time spent in relaxation for slowing the heart rate, cooling down gently, and letting the worked muscles rest naturally. Relaxation is an art (this will be discussed later).

Diet

The basics of life are food, drink, and sleep. Most of us have plenty of the first and second, and too little of the third. We must understand that if we take in more fuel than we burn up we will have an excess — and that means unwanted inches.

Stop and think before taking another potato, or another cup of coffee with sugar. Tell your stomach it doesn't need so much food — it will soon respond. Put a little less on your plate; you will have less waste and very soon a smaller waist line.

Start early — fat children make fat adults.

Cut down on tea, coffee, and too much alcohol. Drink more water and see the results in a clearer skin as the water flushes out your kidneys.

Get plenty of sleep; give yourself time to unwind before going to bed.

What to Wear

Dress comfortably; don't try to exercise in jeans or tight clothing. A leotard and tights or catsuit, or even a tee shirt over a pair of tights, are fine. The important thing is that you are unrestricted and warm.

Leg warmers, ankle warmers, and tights are strongly recommended as they keep the muscles warm and cut down the risk of pulls and strains. They are not just meant to look good; they play an important part in preventing injury. They also prevent warm muscles from cooling down too quickly, again helping to prevent straining.

Wear ballet shoes or exercise in bare feet,

whichever is most comfortable.

After exercising wrap up well, cool down slowly by relaxing as explained at the end of the exercise section and you need never feel stiff, catch a chill or strain anything.

Don't wear jewellery that is likely to catch on anything. Nasty accidents can happen with dangling earrings or necklaces.

Pain

If it hurts — STOP. There are two different types of pain. There is the stiffness that we get when we exercise vigorously after having done very little for a long time. This means your body is working hard — enjoy it. A warm bath will work wonders. Then there is injury pain that is sharp and stabbing. Don't make unreasonable demands on your body. Start slowly and gently, build up to a level that you can maintain, and then work to improve as you see the results.

If you follow the instructions for warming up, dress properly, and relax after exercising you will never injure yourself.

Walk Tall

Stand up straight, tuck your bottom in, pull your tummy in and walk tall. Throw your legs forward from the hips and slink. You will look good, feel fantastic — and just wait for the admiring glances.

Before Exercising

Always make sure you have an empty
bladder. Don't eat a heavy meal or drink
alcohol. This could result in cramp and
nausea.

Check List

If you have any heart condition,
hypertension, or serious varicose veins you
should consult your doctor as to the level of
exercise he considers sensible for you.

Listen to your body. If anything hurts —
stop.

Pay special attention to all exercises
involving your back. Start very gently, build
up gradually. NEVER STRAIN.

Exercising should be fun as well as
beneficial. So make sure you enjoy the
movements, and choose music that you can
sing along to.

How to Use This Book

To do all the exercises in this book will take
one hour. This is your goal. Start slowly and
work your way up. Use the book to suit your
needs and daily routine. DON'T TRY TOO
MUCH TOO SOON. Be sensible; begin carefully;
build up the number of repetitions and the
length of time you do each exercise *until you
reach the ideal*.

You will see a box at the top of each page. This is to give you the *ideal* number of repeats or length of time for each of the exercises.

The boxes also contain suggested music. A good idea is to have your music on a cassette tape; this can run continuously and save you changing records.

Warm~up

(1)

(2)

Stand up tall, tummy and bottom tucked well in, and WALK, stretching your arms above your head in a circular motion. Continue for a minute or two — then lift the knee and extend the leg in front of you (1) (2). Now skip, lifting the knee as high as possible (3). Then trot, point your toes, and keep going for as long as you can. Breath in through your nose and out through your mouth; this will stop you gasping.

WARM UP:	5 minutes

MUSIC
SUGGESTION: 'That's All' — Genesis
'Wide Boy' — Nik Kershaw

(4)

(3)

(5)

You should warm up for at least five minutes.

As a variation try jumping on the spot, swing from one foot to the other sideways and from front to back **(4) (5)**.

You should now be feeling warm, your heart beating steadily and evenly and eager for more.

Loosen~up

(6)

(6a)

Get rid of stiffness in the back and legs

Start by toe touching, bending over and touching the right foot with the left hand **(6)**, then to the other side **(6a)**. Then with both hands to the floor between your legs **(7)** push down three times and stretch up **(8)**.

	IDEAL
TOE TOUCHES	**16**
2 HANDS OVER	**16**
FOLD IN HALF	**16**
MUSIC SUGGESTION: '1999' — Prince	
	'Love and Pride' — King

(7)

(8)

Don't worry if you need to bend your knees for the first few times: this soon won't be necessary. Use bouncy music; make it fun.

Next take both hands over to each foot. Then, feet together, and fold in half.

Waist Trimmer

(9)

Keeping your back straight, bend from the waist to the right pushing your arm down your leg. Do this four times

Now push to the left four times **(9)** . Then push from side to side eight times. You should feel it pulling and trimming your waist.

	IDEAL
WAIST TRIMMER	8
ARM OUTSTRETCHED	4
HANDS BEHIND HEAD	4

MUSIC   'Easy Lover' — **Phil Collins/Phil Bailey**
SUGGESTION: 'Frankie' — **Sister Sledge**

(10)

(11)

Try the same exercise with your arm outstretched **(10)** and again with the hands behind your head **(11)**.

It won't be long before you can combine the toe touching and waist trimming and find it easier to sustain for longer periods.

Waist **S**tretch

(12)

(12a)

Stand with feet apart and push from the waist to the right side, taking your left arm over your head. Push four times. Then take the right arm over and push to the left four times. Do this at least twelve times **(12) (12a)**.

	IDEAL
WAIST STRETCH	**12**
HOLDING HIP	**12**
PALM UP	**12**
MUSIC	**'Easy Lover' — Phil Collins/Phil Bailey**
SUGGESTION:	**'Frankie' — Sister Sledge**

(13)

(14)

Try the same exercise but hold your hip with the opposite arm **(13)**. Repeat twelve times.

Release the hip and take the right hand over the head and push from the waist, this time with the palm of your hand facing the ceiling **(14)**. Do this twelve times.

Thighs

(15)

A lovely simple exercise. Jump and lift your knee as high as you can **(15),** one leg then the other. Swing your arms freely and enjoy it.

Next, jump your feet apart, and then jump them together. Do four with your arms by your side and four taking the arms out with the legs to form an 'X' **(16) (17).**

	IDEAL
KNEES UP	**64**
JUMPS	**12**

MUSIC   'Harden My Heart' — Quarterflash
SUGGESTION: 'American Heartbeat' — Survivor

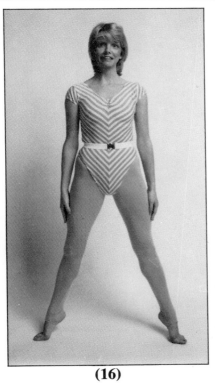

(16)

(17)

Keep going for as long as you can, but remember the golden rule: *if it hurts STOP!*

Try to remember to breathe in through your nose and out through your mouth, and to have a good wriggle of the arms and legs between each of the exercises. It will help to prevent stiffness and tightening of muscles.

Arm Swings

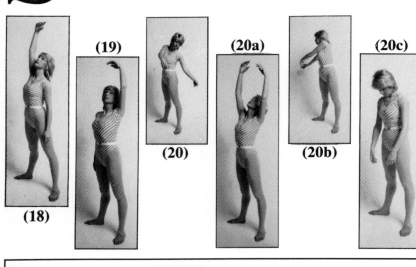

(19)

(20a)

(20c)

(20)

(20b)

(18)

	IDEAL
ARM SWINGS	12
MUSIC	'Harden My Heart' — Quarterflash
SUGGESTION:	'American Heartbeat' — Survivor

Stand comfortably with the feet apart. Swing the right arm from the shoulder *backwards* three times **(18)**, then the left arm **(19)**. Next throw both arms in a circular movement in front of your face — three to the right and three to the left **(20)**.

Bust Toner

	IDEAL
BUST TONER:	**24**
AGAINST WALL	**5**
GRIPPING WRISTS	**20**

NO MUSIC REQUIRED

(22)

(21)

(23)

Stand with the feet apart. Place finger tips on shoulders and draw circles in the air with your elbows in a backwards direction **(21)**.

Lean against a wall, with your legs straight and your arms stretched above your head. Press your arms against the wall, pushing your chest and stomach forward. Relax, then repeat five times **(22)**.

Grip your wrists firmly and hold them at shoulder height. Force your hands to slide up your forearms to your elbows. Do this for at least twenty counts **(23)**.

Floor Work

(24)

(25)

Lie down on a mat or a thick towel; not only does this cushion your back, it also stops you sliding about, especially if you are on a polished floor. For a few seconds lie flat and relax. Let everything go!

Try to tighten each of your muscles separately. Work through your calves, thighs, and tummy (try to pull in the lower pelvic area separately to your tummy). Then really pull in your buttocks. If you are pulling tightly enough you will feel them quiver.

Remember, DON'T STRAIN. Do all the exercises at your own pace — build up gradually. However, don't be lazy. Make your body work.

	IDEAL
SIT UPS	12
HANDS ON HIPS	12
HANDS BEHIND HEAD	12

MUSIC   'I Wanna Know Where Love Is' —
SUGGESTION: Foreigner
              'Friends' — Ami Stewart

(27)

(26)

Lie flat on your back. Sit up, stretching your arms above your head (24). This will lift your diaphragm and pull up any extra inches you may have (temporarily!). Fold in half, putting your head on your knees, and take hold of your feet (25). Repeat twelve times if you can.

Now try sitting up with your hands on your hips (26).

Next place your hands behind your head and sit up (27). You will find this hard to start with. Always come up through a curved spine and try not to pull with your hands on your neck. It soon becomes easier.

If you find it hard to do this try anchoring your feet. Hook them under the bed, or ask someone to hold them for you.

Tummy Toners

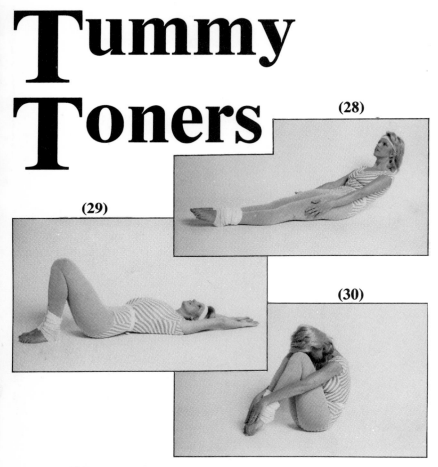

(28)

(29)

(30)

Lie flat, hands by your side and touching your legs. Slowly raise head and shoulders off the ground and slide your hands down towards your knees. Hold for a few seconds and slowly lower to the floor. Don't sit up. You should be at a 45° angle to the floor **(28)**.

Lie flat, knees up, with feet on the floor close to your bottom. Stretch your arms above your head **(29)**. Pull up, swinging your arms over your head to touch your toes and

	IDEAL
PULL UPS	12
TRIANGLE	12
ARMS OUTSTRETCHED	8
SIT UPS	8
MUSIC SUGGESTION:	**'I Wanna Know Where Love Is' — Foreigner 'Friends' — Ami Stewart**

(31)

(32)

(33)

(34)

form a triangle **(30)**. Let your heels come off the ground. Relax back to the floor. Repeat for as long as is comfortable.

Lie flat, legs straight, arms outstretched **(31)**. Sit up, keeping the arms out and at shoulder height **(32)**, then lower to rhe floor.

Lie flat, knees up, feet apart **(33)**. Sit up, pulling forward with your arms **(34)**. Lower and relax. Repeat for as long as is comfortable.

Tummy and Thighs

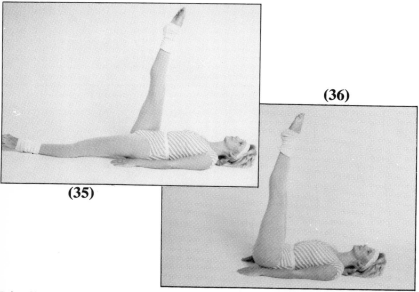

(36)

(35)

Lie flat, hands either by your side or supporting your lower back. Lift one leg at a time quite slowly **(35)**. Then lift both legs together **(36)**. Lower them nearly to the ground but don't let them touch the floor. Lift them up again, and then lower to the ground. Do this five times, then rest for a few seconds.

Now try the same exercise again but at half the speed. You

	IDEAL
LEG LIFTS	**10**
SLOW LIFTS	**8**
MUSIC	**'Penny Lover' — Lionel Ritchie**
SUGGESTION:	**'One More Night' — Phil Collins**

(37)

will feel it pulling on your tummy and thighs. The slower the exercise, the greater the results. Build up your strength and control; don't strain, and don't be in too much of a hurry.

When you can manage the leg lifting easily try putting your hands under your head (37).

Legs

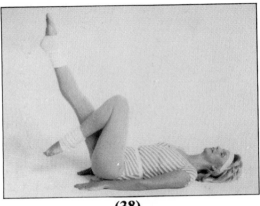

(38)

(39)

Lie flat, hands cushioning the base of your spine. Lift legs off the floor and cycle **(38)**. Keep going for as long as you can (see Box for ideal).

Try cycling with your hands behind your head (you may find

	IDEAL
CYCLING	**100**
HANDS BEHIND HEAD	**50**
KNEES IN AND OUT	**20**

MUSIC SUGGESTION: 'Too Late for Goodbyes' — Julian Lennon
'Easy Lover' — Phil Collins/Phil Bailey

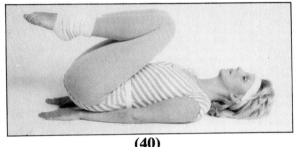

(40)

(41)

this quite difficult to start with) **(39)**.

Lie flat, draw knees up to chest **(40)**, then extend legs straight out as close to the floor as possible. Repeat as much as you can **(41)**.

Thighs

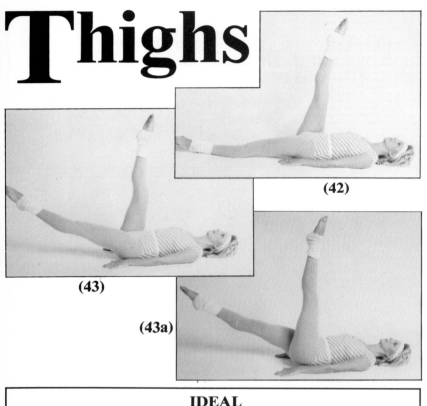

(42)

(43)

(43a)

	IDEAL
LEG CHANGES	**50**
MUSIC SUGGESTION:	**'Too Late for Goodbyes' — Julian Lennon** **'Easy Lover' — Phil Collins/Phil Bailey**

Lie flat, hands by your side, one leg in the air **(42)**. Change legs in mid air **(43)**. Keep your tummy pulled in and your toes pointed.

Once you can do this comfortably try putting your hands under your head, or place the hands on your tummy.

General Stretch

(44)

(45)

(46)

	IDEAL
STRETCH AND ROLL	6
MUSIC SUGGESTION:	'Private Dancer' — Tina Turner 'Can't Slow Down' — Lionel Ritchie

Pull up onto your shoulders and support your back **(44)**. Really stretch your legs up. Bring knees to head **(45)**, stretch up, knees to head, then stretch. Roll into a sitting position and fold in half **(46)**. Roll back up onto shoulders and repeat five times. You should aim for a fluid and even rhythm.

Hips and Bottom

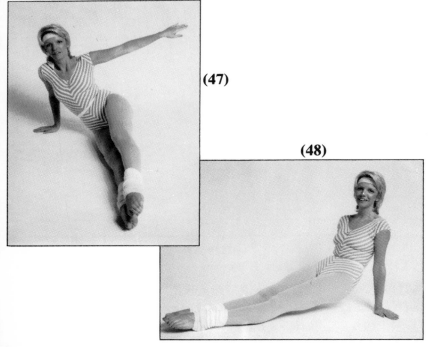

(47)

(48)

This couldn't be easier. Simply roll on your hips and bottom, distributing your weight over the offending parts **(47)**. Then bounce on your bottom and just keep going **(48)**. Walk yourself forward on your bottom, then back again. Now on the spot.

	IDEAL
HIP ROLL	**50**
BOUNCE	**50**
ROCK	**20**
MUSIC	**'Home By the Sea' — Genesis**
SUGGESTION:	**'Let it all Blow' — Dazz Band**

(49)

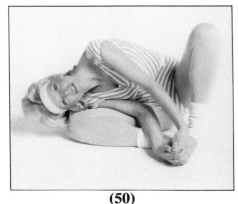

(50)

(50a)

Put the soles of your feet together **(49)**. Hold your feet and rock from side to side. Keep your weight well forward to prevent toppling over **(50)**.

Bottom

(51)

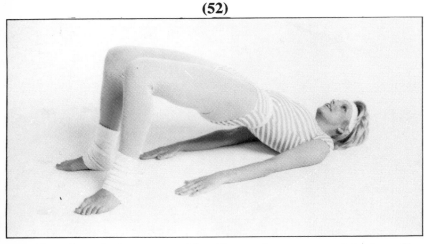

(52)

Lie flat, hands by your side. Draw knees up with feet flat **(51)**. Lift your body up high so that your tummy and thighs form a 'table' **(52)**. Repeat twenty times.

	IDEAL
LIFTS	**20**
CLOSING KNEES	**20**
MUSIC	**'Home By the Sea' — Genesis**
SUGGESTION:	**'Let it all Blow' — Dazz Band**

(53)

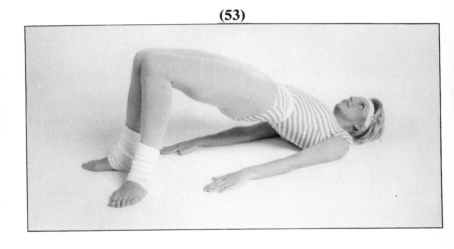

Now try lifting your body closing knees together **(53)**. Lower and at the same time relax the knees. Repeat twenty times. You will be thrilled how well it works.

Thighs and Tummy

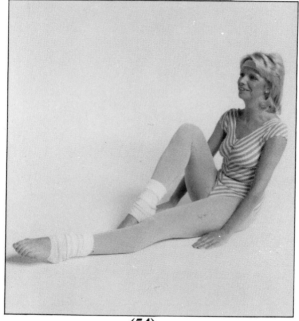

(54)

Sit up straight, legs stretched out in front, toes pointed. Bring
one knee up at a time, making sure to keep your back straight
(54). Do this twenty times slowly and then twenty times as
quickly as you can. Give your legs a good wriggle.

	IDEAL	
LEG CHANGES		
	SLOWLY	**20–40**
	QUICKLY	**20–60**
LEG LIFTS		**6 on each leg**
MUSIC	'View to a Kill' — Duran Duran	
SUGGESTION:	'The Word Girl' — Scritti Pollitti	

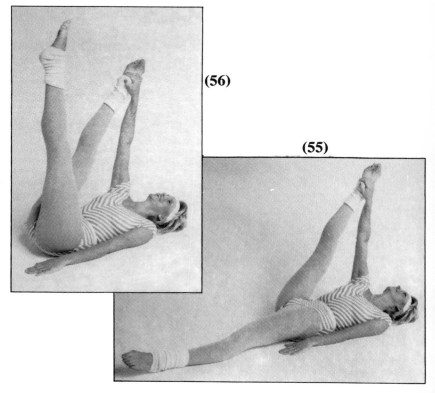

(56)

(55)

Next take hold of the inside of your right foot with your right hand. Stretch it up **(55)**. Support yourself with your left arm. Then lift the left leg to meet the right one **(56)**. Do this six times, then change legs.

Inner Thigh Stretch

(57)

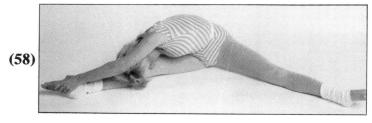

(58)

Sit with your back straight, feet as wide apart as is comfortable. Pull your tummy in. Take your right hand over to your left foot **(57)**. Then left hand to right foot **(58)**. Now fold in half **(59)**. Push three times and sit up straight. Repeat ten times. You will feel it pulling at your hamstrings, but very

	IDEAL
TOE TOUCHING	16
2 HANDS TO EACH FOOT	16
FOLD IN HALF	16

MUSIC SUGGESTION: 'You're Taking It All Too Hard' — Genesis
'View to a Kill' — Duran Duran

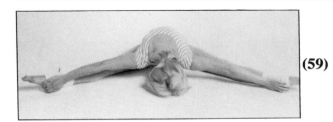

(59)

(60)

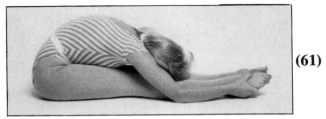

(61)

soon you will be able to put your head on the floor between your legs.

You can also take both hands over to each foot **(60)**.

Then place legs together and fold in half **(61)**.

Hamstring Stretch

(62)

Sit up straight and take hold of your leg underneath the knee **(62)**. Gently extend the leg, pointing your toes **(63)**. Stretch the other leg in the same way and then try both legs together, keeping the weight forward and off the base of the spine **(64)** **(64a)**.

Once the legs will stretch easily try rotating your feet in both directions, and up and down.

	IDEAL
HAMSTRING STRETCH	6 on each leg
BOTH TOGETHER	4
MUSIC SUGGESTION:	'Somebody's Eyes' — Karla Bonoff 'Round and Around' — Jaki Graham

(63)

(64)

(64a)

For a Supple Back

(65)

(66)

(67)

Roll over onto your tummy and VERY GENTLY push up from the waist **(65)**. Keep your shoulders down and your elbows tucked in. Repeat five times.

Push back onto your knees **(66)** and on back into a tucked position **(67)**, keeping the arms well in front. Push forward and return to the floor **(67a) (67b)**.

Kneel on all fours. Swing your right knee in towards your

	IDEAL
PUSH UPS	5
ONTO KNEES	10
LEG THROWS	5 on each leg
MUSIC SUGGESTION:	'Love Don't Live Here Anymore' — Jimmy Nail 'That Ole Devil Called Love' — Alison Moyet

(67a)

(67b)

(68)

(68a)

face and then throw it straight back behind you **(68)**. Repeat five times and then on the other leg. Be careful not to hit your nose!

Lie flat on your tummy, take hold of your ankles and gently pull up. Do this three times. Be careful — don't strain **(68a)**.

Please remember not to strain and build up carefully and gradually.

Hips and Thighs

(69)

(70)

Lie on your side, keeping your hips well forward. Throw your leg up **(69)**. Keep going for as long as you can. Then repeat on the other side.

Lie on your side, lift leg in the air and flex leg from your knee

	IDEAL
LEG LIFT	50 on each leg
FLEXES	20 on each leg
'V'	3
MUSIC SUGGESTION:	'Axel F' — Harold Faltermeyer 'Illegal Alien' — Genesis

(71)

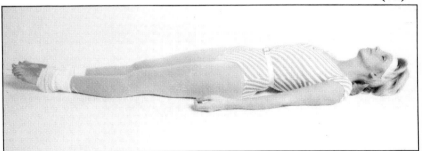

(72)

(70). Repeat twenty times, then roll on to the other side and use the other leg.

Lie flat on your back. Pull up feet and shoulders together to form a 'V' **(71)**. Repeat three times, then lie flat and relax for a few seconds **(72)**. Have a good wriggle before getting up.

Supple Spine

(74)

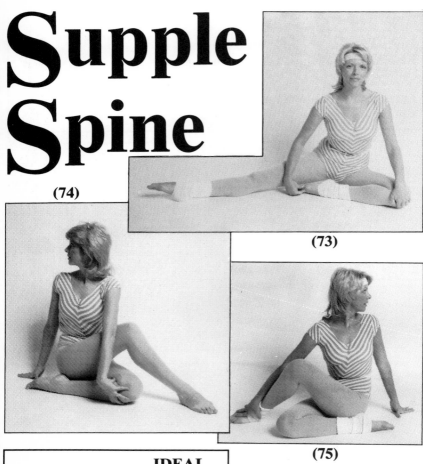

(73)

(75)

	IDEAL
TWISTS	**3 on each side**
NO MUSIC REQUIRED	

Sit up straight and bend the left leg in **(73)**. Put the right leg across the left leg so that your foot is on the floor and your knee is bent. Hold your left knee with your left hand. Put your right hand on the floor and turn towards the right **(74)**. Push gently. Repeat on the other side **(75)**.

Top to Toe Stretch

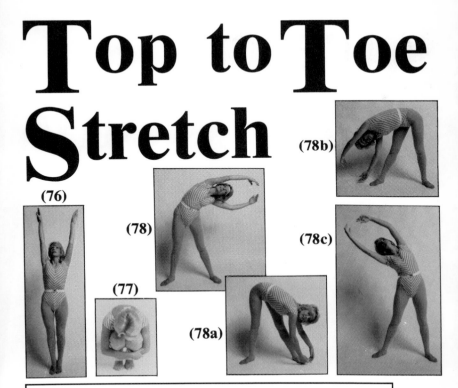

(76)

(77)

(78)

(78a)

(78b)

(78c)

	IDEAL
UP AND DOWN	**16**
SWINGS	**16**
MUSIC	**'Cherish' — Kool and the Gang**
SUGGESTION:	**'Everytime You Go Away' —**
	Paul Young

Pull up onto your toes and stretch your abdomen. Reach up with your hands **(76)**. Bend the knees and crouch down into a little ball **(77)**. Continue up and down.

Swing your arms and body in a circle from the waist, letting your hands touch the floor as you go round **(78)**. First in one direction, and then in the other.

Stretch Your Body

(79)

Stand up straight, hands above your head. Step to the right and bend from the waist towards the left **(79)**. Step feet together. Then step to the left and repeat on the other side. Do twenty of these. This pulls in and trims you beautifully.

	IDEAL
SIDE STEP	**20**
SWINGS	**20**
JUMPS	**20**
MUSIC SUGGESTION:	**'Kayleigh' — Marillion**
	'No More Lonely Nights' — Paul McCartney

(80)

(81)

Swing freely from side to side, stretching as much as you can **(80)**.

Skip and jump in the air going from side to side, lifting your leg as high as you can and aim for good elevation **(81)**.

L^{eg}
S_{wings}

(82)

(83)

Stand straight, arms out to side for balance. Swing the leg up, from the hip, to 90° to the floor **(82)**. Swing leg through behind you as high as you can **(83)**. Keep swinging legs alternately until they tire.

	IDEAL
LEG SWINGS	**30**
KNEE TURN	**30**
MUSIC SUGGESTION:	'Slave to Love' — Bryan Ferry 'This is not America' — David Bowie

(84)

(85)

Lift your knee to the front **(84)**, and turn it to the side **(85)**. This exercise will help you to walk more elegantly. Always remember when you walk to swing your legs from the hip and not from the knee.

Waist Turns

(86)

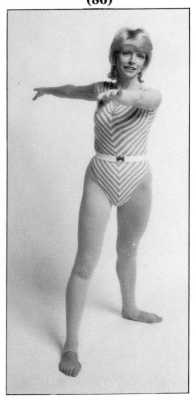

Stand straight, feet apart. Keep your hips and knees perfectly still, arms shoulder height at 90° **(86)**. Swing arms round

	IDEAL
WAIST TURNS	**100**
DOUBLE PUSH	**40**
MUSIC SUGGESTION:	**'Holding Out for a Hero' — Bonnie Tyler**
	'Shout it to the Top' — Style Council

(87)

(88)

from side to side at least twenty times **(87)**. Now try with a double push to each side. Then let your whole body flop **(88)**.

Stretching With a Chair

(89)

(90)

(91)

A chair, or the draining board, can be usefully employed for stretching.

Put your foot on the chair or draining board and stretch up **(89)**. Then fold over your leg **(90)** and down the supporting leg **(91)**.

Take the inside of your foot and gently stretch **(92)** one side, then the other.

Take the foot at the back and gently lift it up **(93)**. Try and keep the supporting leg straight — but don't strain.

(92)

(93)

Cooling Down

COOL DOWN	3 minutes
MUSIC	**'Axel F' — Harold Faltermeyer**
SUGGESTION:	**'History' — Mai Tai**

Cooling down is just as important as warming up. You can do this in several ways but I like to skip or spring around the room. Then trot and gradually slow down to a walk, letting everything relax and then finally flop.

Special Problems

Most women, from time to time, suffer from premenstrual tension, period pains, and headaches. These can be relieved by simple exercises.

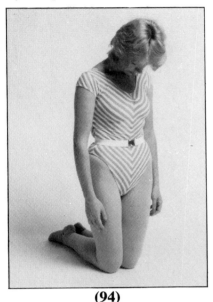

(94)

(95)

TENSION RELIEF

Sit comfortably and let your head roll forward, chin on your chest **(94)**. Gently lift the chin and roll the head back **(95)**.

(96)

(97)

Continue in this way and feel the tension loosen in your neck. Now roll the head to your shoulder **(96)** then to the other side. Repeat this several times. Finally roll the head around **(97)**, first one way then the other.

(98)

(99)

PERIOD PAIN RELIEF

Kneel on all fours, arch the back **(98)**, then let it drop. You should look rather like a cat. Continue arching and dropping and feel the relief.

Lie flat on the floor, arms by your side. Gently push the small of your back onto the floor and release **(99)**. Repeat four or five times.

If you are ever in any doubt about back exercises, DON'T do them.

Relaxation

(100)

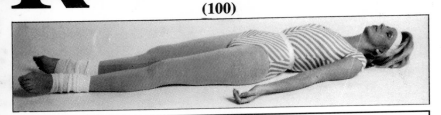

RELAXATION	5–10 Minutes
MUSIC SUGGESTION:	'Gymnopodie 1 and 3' — Erik Satie

This is of paramount importance. After any exercise you must give your body time to slow down and cool down. The heart and pulse need to be allowed to beat normally and we can create an inner calm to help us tackle all the things we have to do.

LIE DOWN, having put on a warm sweater or track suit and some relaxing music, preferably instrumental.

Work your way through all of your limbs, starting with the toes, ankles, calves, and thighs. Feel them release and relax. Continue up, hips, tummy, chest, shoulders, neck, and head; arms, hands, and fingers. Lastly, relax your face. Close your eyes and let yourself float away. Concentrate only on your breathing: in through the nose, hold for eight counts, and let it out through the mouth. Try not to think about anything else. Just drift.

Stay in this state for at least five minutes, or until the music stops. Then have a wriggle, open your eyes, and sit up when you are ready. You will feel wonderful, rested, calm and ready to tackle the rest of the day.